D1636924

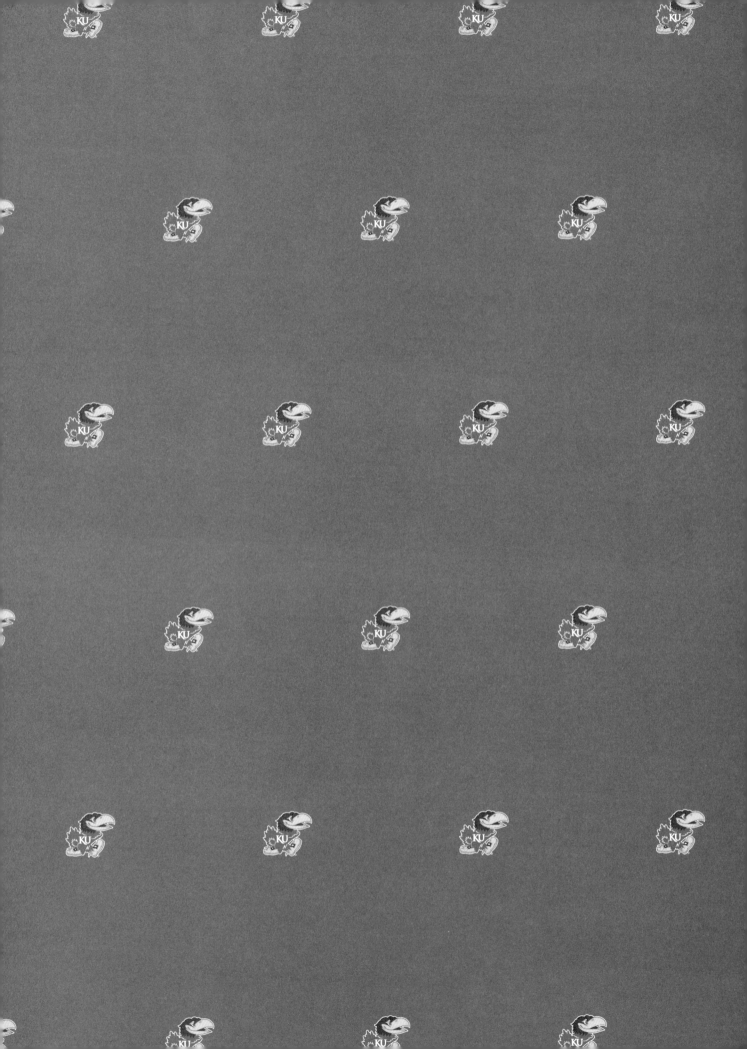

When I Grow Up,
I WANT TO BE A
JAYHAWK

KANSAS

Written and illustrated
by Greg Hardin

To all future (and past and present) Jayhawks,
and for my beloved ladies Ashley and Taylor.
– GH

A SPECIAL THANK YOU TO THESE KICKSTARTER BACKERS!

YOUNG SIGN COMPANY LEAVENWORTH, KS	JD AND ALBERTA BITTEL	ERIN WOODWARD FAMILY CONCIERGE KC
ROCK CHALK BLOG ROCKCHALKBLOG.COM	THE PHOG.NET FORUMS	THE KUSPORTS.NET FORUMS

Will Katz and Michelle Hayes Ruby Katz	Nate, Jen, Andrew and Charlotte Hardin	Jayhawk Nation by Crown Town Media
Josie and RJ Whitsitt Love Mommy and Daddy	Scott and Sheryl Bird	Ed, Katie, George, Jack and Patrick Marx
Elizabeth A. Schartz	Larry Smith and John Scarpate Jayhawk Brothers forever! RCJH	The McRae, Swanson and Higginbotham families
Future Jayhawks: Nikki Reed & Samantha Reed	Alexandrea, Evan and Giulianna Mann	Hazel and Caleb Porter William Wages

© 2016 Big Cheer, LLC
Published by Big Cheer, LLC, Shawnee, Kansas.

First Edition

The Jayhawk Logo is owned by The University of Kansas and is used with permission.

The text for this book is set in Fink Heavy by House Industries.

For more information, visit www.facebook.com/WhenIGrowUpIWantToBeAJayhawk

Printed in Malaysia

ISBN 978-0-692-58887-1
Library of Congress Control Number: 2015921409

Hello citizens, my name is Jay.
But that's just my secret identity, what I call myself today.

I protect you from bad guys, those pains in the neck!

If they try anything around me,
they're gonna hit the deck!

I'm not really a superhero, even though that would rock.

But you know what I could be?
I want to be a Jayhawk!

"What I want to be when I grow up"

I want to go to that beautiful school up on the hill,
where the great big sunflowers grow.

In awesome Lawrence, Kansas,
the greatest college town you'll ever get to know!

Did you know astronauts, Olympians, senators and governors went to KU?

Actors, Hall of Famers, Nobel
Prize and Pulitzer winners did too!

Who else goes to KU?
People of all sizes and shapes!

I can't wait to make new friends,
from a hundred countries and all 50 states!

Whoa, what is this interrupting my rhyme?
It's the Marching Jayhawks! It must be halftime!

It'll be so much fun to live in a dorm
or a house, choosing what to eat!

Being on my own for the first time
is going to be so sweet!

My curiosity is enormous,
I want to explore the unknown.

There will be so much to learn
from the teachers and on my own!

I can study to be an engineer or a scientist!
A teacher, lawyer or musician!

I can't list them all, but how about
an architect, journalist or physician?

Here I am at KU's famous palace of basketball,
where some say their royal blood is blue.

Maybe if I work hard enough,
I'll grow up to be a Kansas legend too!

And if not, I can still Wave the Wheat
or sing the Rock Chalk Chant;
so many traditions to fulfill.

The greatest of all will be when I graduate
and get to walk down the Hill!

So many came before me,
with their discoveries,
honors, championships and awards.

I want to earn my degree and be just like them,
they're the examples I look toward.

To be great there,
you don't need to crash from another planet
or travel a yellow brick road.

Just dream big and work really hard
and all of your super-ness will show!

I want to grow up to be a Jayhawk,
and wear that crimson and blue.
I hope someday I'll see you there!
ROCK CHALK JAYHAWK, KU!

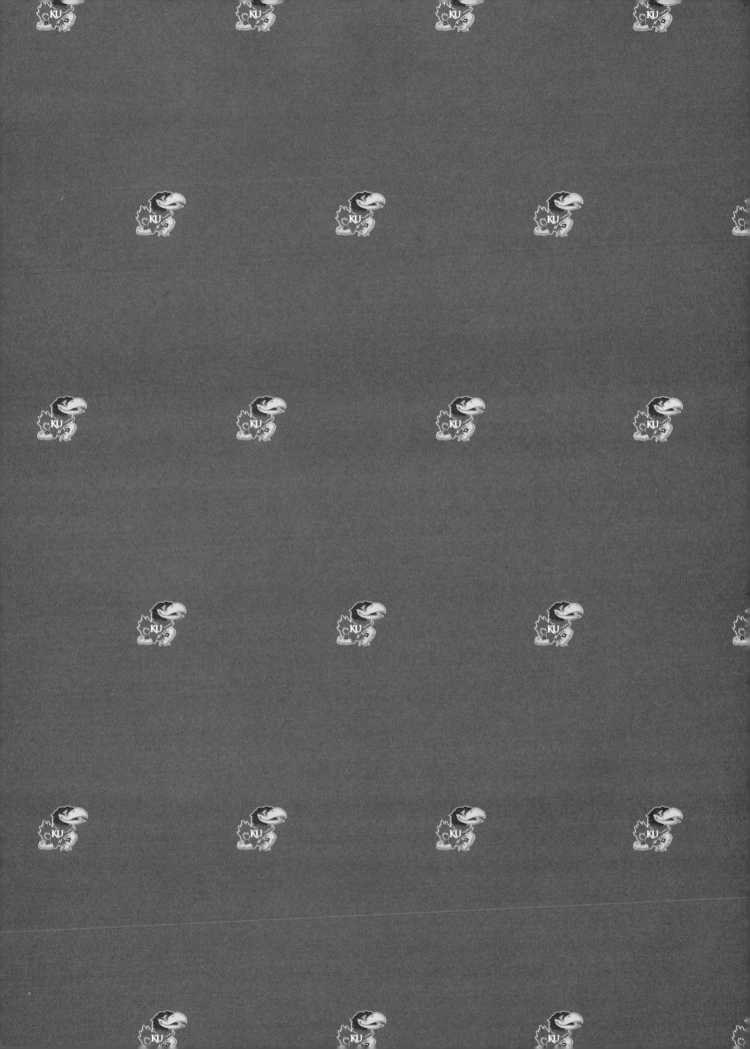